DATE DUE

Thomas Alva Edison

Brian Williams

Heinemann Library
Chicago, Illinois

Designed by AMR
Originated by Ambassador Litho
Printed in Hong Kong/China

05 04 03 02 01
10 9 8 7 6 5 4 3 2 1

Library of Congress Cataloging-in-Publication Data
Williams, Brian, 1959-
    Thomas Alva Edison / Brian Williams.
        p. cm. – (Groundbreakers)
    Includes bibliographical references and index.
    Summary: A biography of the inventor who changed the world in which he lived with
such revolutionary inventions as the phonograph, electric lighting, and motion picture.
    ISBN 1-57572-377-8 (library)
    1. Edison, Thomas A. (Thomas Alva), 1847-1931—Juvenile literature. 2.
Inventors—United States—Biography—Juvenile literature. 3. Electric engineers—United
States—Biography—Juvenile literature. [1. Edison, Thomas A. (Thomas Alva),
1847-1931. 2. Inventors.] I. Title. II. Series.

TK140.E3 W47 2000
621.3'092—dc21
[B]   00-021098

Acknowledgments
The Publishers would like to thank the following for permission to reproduce photographs:
Bridgeman Art Library, p. 4; Edison National Historic Site, pp. 5, 6, 7, 8, 12, 14, 16, 17, 19, 20,
21, 22, 23, 24, 26, 27, 28, 31, 32, 34, 35, 36, 37, 38, 39, 40, 41; Hulton Getty, pp. 9, 33; Mary
Evans Picture Library, pp. 10, 25, 29; Science Museum/Science & Society Picture Library, p. 11;
Peter Newark's Military Pictures, p. 13; Robert Harding Picture Library, pp. 15, 42; Corbis,
pp. 18, 30, 43.

Cover photograph reproduced with permission of Edison National Historic Site.

Every effort has been made to contact copyright holders of any material reproduced in this
book. Any omissions will be rectified in subsequent printings if notice is given to the publisher.

Some words are shown in bold, **like this.** You can find out what
they mean by looking in the glossary.

Contents

The Man who Made the Future

Switch on the light. Night turns into day. Now think of a few other ways in which we use electricity—television, computers, tools, gadgets, electric trains…the list is enormous. We live in a "plugged in" world.

Edison's world

Not much more than 100 years ago, life was very different. There were steam trains, and steam engines in factories, but the power of steam couldn't provide light. At nightfall, it became very dark. Townspeople lit hissing gas lamps. In the countryside, smelly oil lanterns and flickering candles gave patches of light. Most people went to bed soon after it got dark.

Daily life was different, too. People did business and exchanged news by writing letters, because there were no telephones. They entertained themselves by talking, playing games, reading, singing, and dancing. There were no radios, no stereos, no films, and no television.

When Edison was born, most people lit their homes by candles and oil lamps. After dark, they sat in pools of light, surrounded by flickering shadows and dark corners, as shown in this painting by Johannes Rosiere (1818–1901). Today, most people use candles only when there is a power outage.

What Edison did

Thomas Edison gave the world electric light, sound recording, and moving pictures—marvels that we now take for granted. In his lifetime, he came up with more than 1,000 inventions or ideas for inventions. They included business aids, vote recorders, an electric pen, a talking doll, a magnetic "iron-finder," better **batteries,** electric trains and cars, and even helicopters and concrete houses. He built the first electricity generating station, lit city streets, improved the telephone, and created one of the most successful businesses in the U.S. Some other inventors died poor and frustrated, but not Edison. Inventing made him rich and famous. People all over the world knew his name.

Edison was more than a dreamer; he was a practical engineer who turned ideas into money, often improving other people's inventions. Sometimes he failed, but not for lack of effort. All his life he was **optimistic** and determined, sometimes ruthless, always hard-working. His example inspired many Americans, and his research methods were copied the world over. In many ways, Edison helped to create the modern world.

Edison proudly holds one of his early electric light bulbs. Inventing an instant, yet constant, source of light changed the way people lived and worked. By the time this photograph was taken, Edison was probably the most famous inventor in the world.

Early Life

Like many other Americans in the mid-nineteenth century, Samuel and Nancy Edison were trying to bring up a family and make a better life for themselves in a changing world. Nancy was interested in books and ideas, while Sam's thoughts drifted more towards new business ventures, which were seldom very successful.

Edison was born on February 11, 1847, in the small town of Milan, Ohio. At that time, the United States of America were not yet fully explored. The West was still wild, and many people were new arrivals.

Edison's father, Samuel, a small-time businessman, had moved south from Canada in the 1830s. He and his wife Nancy, a teacher, settled in Milan. Three of the Edisons' first six children died young, and the oldest were teenagers when a seventh child was born in 1847. He was named Thomas Alva, but the family called him Al.

Since his brother and two sisters were much older, Al played mostly on his own. He found it hard to make friends because he did not hear well—the problem may have been caused by scarlet fever. By the time he was twelve, he later recalled, he was "too deaf to hear birds sing."

Childhood and changing times

As a child, Al learned how to fill oil lamps, chop firewood, and feed the horse. He walked with his mother to the town stores and went to bed by candlelight as darkness and silence fell over the small town. Nothing much changed until he was seven, when the Edisons' lives were turned upside down. It was time for them to move.

In 1853, a new railroad bypassed their town. Trade followed the trains away from Milan, and its stores were hit hard. Samuel Edison, never successful in land and timber buying, decided it was time to move to a new life in Port Huron, Michigan.

The struggling schoolboy

At his new home, a small river port beside Lake Huron, Al went to school, but he did not do well in class. He could not hear well and asked so many questions that the bad-tempered teacher told Mrs. Edison that Al was "addled"—mixed-up and no good. His father had always thought he was stupid.

Nancy Edison knew he wasn't, and she took him out of school. She taught him at home, reading with him the plays of William Shakespeare and the writings of the ancient Greek **philosophers.** Al never wrote or spelled well, however, nor was he good at math.

The Scottish engineer James Watt did not invent the steam engine, but his work in the 1760s and 1770s had turned a pumping engine that was not very efficient into a machine that could drive all kinds of machinery. The factories and mills of Edison's boyhood used steam power for all the jobs that were too tough for horsepower or human muscles. There were even steam plows on farms. Children like Edison built model steam engines the way children today build model cars or planes.

What Al was brilliant at was making things. His favorite reading at age nine was a book of science experiments, and he persuaded his mother to let him set up a **laboratory** in his bedroom. There he often worked at night, by candlelight, dreaming. If only there was a way to turn night into day. A man could make his fortune….

Al spent the first seven years of his life in this red brick house in Milan, Ohio. It was a comfortable but not luxurious home. Today, the house where Edison was born is a museum.

Working the Railroad

This photograph of Al at the age of fourteen shows a cheerful, confident young man, already in business on his own. Could anyone have predicted the fame that awaited this determined teenager?

Mrs. Edison soon banished the young scientist and his smelly chemicals to the cellar. Neighbors watched nervously for new oddities and developments at the Edison place. Al rigged up a **battery**-powered **telegraph,** stringing wires from trees to a friend's house. He built miniature steam engines that hissed, rattled, and sometimes exploded!

To earn money for chemicals and spare parts, ten-year-old Al sold tickets to tourists who came to view Lake Huron from a rickety tower his father had built. He also sold vegetables grown by a friend, driving around town in the family's horse and cart to deliver them.

In business

In 1859, the new Grand Trunk Railroad linked Port Huron with Detroit. For Al, this was more than just the chance to ride a steam train every day. It was a business opportunity.

It was a three-hour train ride into Detroit. Young Al talked his way on board, selling newspapers, sweets, snacks, and other items to the passengers. He had to buy his own supplies, but he could keep all the money he made. The Edisons needed the money because Al's father's grain and timber business was not doing well. Many other children his age were working, and Al was delighted to be his own boss.

He got on the morning train at 7:00 A.M., spent the day in Detroit, and came home on the 6:30 P.M. train. The train conductor agreed to let him set up his **laboratory** in the train's baggage car, so he could carry out experiments while the train waited in Detroit for the return trip.

Al also hung around the city telegraph office, talking to the operators as messages came clicking in and out across the wires. He was fascinated. This was an amazing new world waiting for him.

Young Al could not buy the small "dry" batteries we use today in personal stereos, watches, and flashlights. The battery he used in his telegraph was "wet," containing chemicals and metal plates. A chemical reaction caused a **current** to flow from one plate to another. Batteries were the only way to store electricity. The first battery was made by an Italian named Alessandro Volta in about 1800.

The railroad gave Al his first business opportunity. The first steam railroad in the United States began in 1831. The U.S. government encouraged railroad building to aid settlement of the West, and by 1869, tracks spanned the country from coast to coast.

Messages by Wire

The **telegraph** that so fascinated young Al Edison was transforming communications. For the first time, signals could be sent further than the eye could see, at incredible speed.

The telegraph used the new, and still only half-understood, power of electricity. In 1820, the Danish scientist Hans Christian Oersted found that the electric **current** from a **battery** could make a **magnetized** needle move. In 1831, the English scientist Michael Faraday made an equally important discovery. He found that moving a magnet through a coil of wire caused an electric current to flow through the wire.

These breakthroughs in what is known as **"electromagnetism"** made it possible to build electric motors (machines that moved because of electricity) and **generators** (machines that made electricity by moving). They also gave scientists the idea of creating a "code" for sending messages by using changes in the way electricity traveled.

The first telegraphs

Samuel Morse built the first successful telegraph in 1837, with the help of a New York University friend, Leonard Gale. With the assistance of Alfred Vail, Morse then worked out a code in which dots and dashes stood for letters of the alphabet.

In 1844, Vail and Morse amazed U.S. senators by telegraphing a message along a line from Washington, D.C. to Baltimore. The message sped along the wire faster than an express train.

The telegraph brought a revolution in communication. This picture shows telegraphists in Italy, in 1897. The first telegraph across the Atlantic in 1866 brought almost instant communication between the U.S. and Europe.

By 1851, there were more than 50 telegraph companies in the United States. Newspapers used the telegraph to gather news, and businesses sent money "by wire" or checked the latest stock market prices. When the American Civil War began in 1861, the telegraph was a vital link between armies. The "humming wires" strung between poles soon linked most towns, following the railways across prairies and mountains.

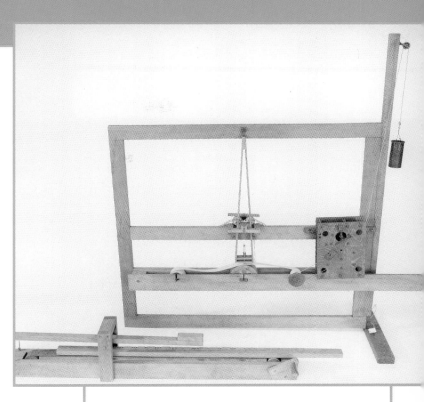

*The first telegraph made by Samuel Morse was **patented** in 1837. Messages were sent by tapping a key which completed and broke the electrical circuit. In **Morse code,** the electrical stops and starts became dots and dashes, heard as clicks as the telegraph tapped out messages.*

Electricity comes of age

Edison read all he could about electricity. He must have been inspired by reading about Michael Faraday. Like Edison, Faraday never went to college, but learned his science as an assistant to the English chemist Humphry Davy. In earlier times, electricity had been a mysterious magic, used in weird medical treatments and in machines that crackled with sparks and gave shocks if people touched them!

Faraday made the study of electricity a science, with its own laws. As Edison grew up, other scientists were taking up the challenge and revealing the enormous powers of electromagnetism. The pieces of the jigsaw puzzle were falling into place. A new technology was coming.

In Edison's words:

While Al was looking after his train business, he was also expanding his trading empire. *"I started two stores in Port Huron, one for periodicals [magazines] and the other for vegetables, butter, and berries in the season. They were attended by two boys who shared in the profits."*

Tramp Telegrapher

In 1861, the Civil War began. This war between the Northern and Southern states was the biggest news story in years. People were desperate to read about the latest battles, and newspaper editors relied on the **telegraph** to get the latest reports from the battlefields. It was the first test for the new technology.

In 1862, a bloody battle was fought at Shiloh, Tennessee. Al, still only fifteen, watched as the wires began to hum with news of the battle and saw a chance to boost his sales. His friend, a Detroit telegrapher, agreed to wire news flashes along the railway. Al arranged for eye-catching headlines to be chalked on boards at stations, such as, "11,000 die on Union side."

*This page is from Al's **railroad** newspaper, the Grand Trunk Herald, dated February 3, 1862. By then, the Civil War had been going on for almost a year. The newspaper carried war news, as well as advertisements for goods and farm produce.*

Al bought one thousand copies of the newspaper, which carried full reports of the battle, and sold the whole lot on the train's return trip—at more than double the usual price.

In Edison's words:

Edison became a very fast telegrapher. One day he got into a race with a telegrapher in New York, each stepping up the pace until Edison triumphed and wired to his rival, *"'Say, young man, change off and send with your other foot!'"*

From newspaperman to telegrapher

Al made enough money to buy a small printing press, which he set up on the train. The *Grand Trunk Herald,* which he wrote and printed, was probably the first paper ever produced on a railway train. All went well until fire broke out in Al's **laboratory,** and the baggage car attendant told him to find somewhere else to do his experiments. Al kept on selling papers from the stations, but he wanted to try something new.

He took up telegraphy. The story goes that he saved a child from being run down by a train and was rewarded with free dinners and, even better, lessons in telegraphy from the child's father, a telegrapher. Soon the student was faster than his teacher. Al was in his element. It was like someone today learning to surf the Internet.

Making his own equipment, Al became Port Huron's telegraph operator. He became a wizard with the clicking telegraph, possibly because he "could not hear other and perhaps distracting sounds." Sometimes messages were ignored: Al was in the basement, doing experiments!

> THE CIVIL WAR
>
> The Civil War (1861–1865) almost tore apart the United States. It was fought between the Northern states (the Union), and those Southern states that wanted to break away and set up their own republic (the Confederacy). The main issue dividing the two sides was slavery. The Civil War was the first war in which railroads and telegraphs played a key part. Over half a million soldiers died, about half from disease. The North won the war, and slavery was ended.

Into the wide world

At sixteen, Al decided it was time to leave home. Starting in 1863, he traveled the country for five years as a "tramp telegrapher." It was a free, easy life. Al liked to work nights, reading science books by day or rigging up gadgets to amuse himself. One device killed ra s with electric shocks!

This is a Northern army telegraph wagon. The Civil War was the first war in which the telegraph was used, and both sides sent out units like this to string up telegraph wires. Young telegraphers like Al Edison were in demand to deal with the flood of news from the battlefields.

13

The Young Inventor

In 1868, Thomas Edison found himself in Boston. He loved city life, and got a job with Western Union, the leading U.S. **telegraph** company. The scruffily dressed youngster quickly showed that he could take the fastest incoming messages. He could cause trouble, too. Edison wrote in very tiny handwriting when copying long newspaper reports. When scolded for writing so small, he responded the next day by writing in page-size letters!

In Boston, he lived with a telegraph instrument-maker and worked in his spare time on his first invention—a push-button vote recorder, for politicians to vote "yes" or "no" in the U.S. **Congress.** Unfortunately, the politicians were not ready for push-button voting. It was a useful lesson—no invention sells without demand for it. Edison was not dismayed. He left his job at the start of 1869, to concentrate on "bringing out inventions."

Edison gets lucky

Edison was sure he could make the telegraph work faster, to send two, four, or even more messages at the same time. His telegraph research led him to design a faster version of the stock ticker, a telegraph that printed prices of business shares. Edison's ticker printed letters as well as figures, and he soon had quite a few customers.

Edison's printing telegraph, or stock ticker, was an improvement of an existing machine. The ticker was much faster than using office boys to dash from one building to another with the latest financial news. The improved ticker was one of his first inventions and grew out of his interest in telegraphy.

In 1869, he decided to try his luck in New York City, the hub of the American business world and just the place for Edison's talents. "Everybody steals in **commerce** and industry," he said later, "but I knew how to steal." He meant he knew what would work and what wouldn't.

He had a contact, a friendly engineer named Frank Pope, who worked for a gold reporting company. Pope let the jobless Edison sleep in the office basement. Edison was in luck. The company's stock ticker broke down and Edison got it working. He was offered a job on the spot.

Within weeks, he had filed **patents** for his improved stock ticker, or printing telegraph. He gave up his job and went into business with Pope as electrical and telegraph engineers. Work flowed in, mostly from Western Union. One day, a boss at the company Gold and Stock made Edison an astounding offer: $40,000 for all the improvements he had been working on. This was a huge sum of money—it could have taken a telegraph operator twenty years or more to earn this much!

Edison later claimed that he took the money in small bills, and had to ask how to open a bank account. With money in the bank, he could really go to work.

The New York Stock Exchange is one of the most important markets in the world. In Edison's time, the Exchange was already the center for deals in gold mines, railroads, shipping lines, steelworks, and many other ventures. People's fortunes could be made—and lost—in the time it took the stock ticker to tick out a string of prices.

THE STOCK TICKER

Stock exchanges are markets where stocks and shares are bought and sold. Stocks are pieces of paper showing that someone has lent money to the government or to a business. Someone buying shares in a business owns part of that business. The New York Stock Exchange, founded in 1792, began using its first stock ticker in 1867. Tickers worked like telegraphs, printing out paper tape on which the latest prices of company shares, gold, wheat, or other items were shown. It was important that the tickers were fast and did not break down!

15

Building a Team

In 1870, Edison, now 23, bought a workshop in Newark, New Jersey, and began making stock tickers. Business grew quickly, and it was good to be making steady money. Though he was always late paying bills, Edison was quick to hire good people. Three skilled helpers became the backbone of his new team—British engineer Charles Batchelor, German mechanic Sigmund Bergmann, and Swiss watchmaker John Kruesi. Edison wrote home to his parents, joking that he was now "a bloated Eastern manufacturer." He was doing well, and he knew it.

The married man

Busy as he was, Edison found time to court Mary Stilwell, who came to work at the Newark factory. She was sixteen. The wedding took place on Christmas Day, 1871. Edison was sad that his mother was missing from the party. Nancy Edison had died earlier that year. Her inventive son knew deep down that he owed her very much.

Work was Edison's first love, even though he was devoted to his wife. There was so much to do. He was busy improving the **telegraph** but still found time to sit down and improve the typewriter. He invented an electric pen, for making duplicates of documents. The pen made holes in a paper sheet, which was then inked, like a stencil, to run off hundreds of copies. It was a great success.

Mary Stilwell, photographed at the age of sixteen, became Edison's first wife. Having met him through work at the Newark factory, Mary knew exactly the kind of "human **dynamo**" she was marrying. The picture of Edison was taken about four years after the marriage, when he was 27 and about to begin his most creative period as an inventor.

The Edison method

When trying to solve a problem, Edison would read every book he could find on the subject, make notes, and then do experiments—hundreds if necessary—until he found a solution. Crouched over his desk, he would scribble away day and night, falling asleep in his chair. At last, there would come a startling yell of triumph, and he would dance around the room, explaining what had to be done.

Edison knew he lacked theoretical knowledge. In 1875, he stumbled across a sparking phenomenon he called "etheric force." This energy beaming through space offered the possibility of a wireless telegraph. However, Edison never followed the trail, which might have led him to **radio** some twenty years before an Italian, Guglielmo Marconi.

He spent more and more time with lawyers, keeping rivals from stealing his inventions or fighting claims that he had taken someone else's ideas. A lot of technology-borrowing was going on, and things were about to get even more furious.

In Edison's words:

In 1873, Edison crossed the Atlantic Ocean by steamship to sell his latest automatic telegraph to the British Post Office. He was not impressed: *"The English are not an inventive people; they don't eat enough pie. To invent, your system must be all out of order and there is nothing that will do that like the good old-fashioned American pie."*

Edison bought his first workshop in Newark, New Jersey. Newark was a growing industrial town, only 8 miles (13 kilometers) from the business center of New York City. Other inventors had already set up businesses there, and this attracted skilled workers to move to Newark to find jobs.

The **telegraph** could send only dots and dashes, not human voices. In March 1876, a Scottish man who taught deaf people in Boston started a technology revolution. His name was Alexander Graham Bell, and he had invented the telephone.

Bell's machine took the telegraph a step further. It changed the **vibrations** of sounds into electrical signals and back again. When one person spoke into his telephone, another could hear the sounds coming from another telephone at the end of the wire. The sound was very faint and could be heard only over short distances, but it worked.

Everyone in the telegraph business was very excited. Western Union, eager to get in on the new technology, hired Edison to examine Bell's telephone and improve it. Money was no object. In the spring of 1876, Edison moved to Menlo Park, a village about 12 miles (20 kilometers) from Newark, but on the **railroad** to New York City. It was little more than a cluster of houses and sheds, but was suggested to Edison as a good site.

The new research center

Edison transformed Menlo Park into the world's first industrial research **laboratory.** He created workshops and storerooms, a two-story laboratory, a separate chemistry laboratory, and a library crammed with technical books.

Bell was only 29 years old when he showed an astonished world his new telephone, or "far-speaker." The telephone was demonstrated at a Philadelphia exhibition celebrating 100 years of American independence. British scientist Lord Kelvin called it "the most wonderful thing in America." Edison, also 29, was soon claiming that honor for himself.

The Edison family

Menlo Park became the center of Edison's world. Busy with his work, he often saw little of his wife. They already had a daughter, Marion (born in 1873), and at Menlo Park two sons were born, Thomas (1876) and William (1878). Edison was fond of his children, but his other "family" was equally important. They were his team—Batchelor, Kruesi, and the twenty or so other workers who had followed him from the Newark workshop to Menlo Park.

Mrs. Edison had seen the team at work in Newark, and she knew what kind of man her husband was. But even she surely never dreamed that soon he would be world famous as "the Wizard of Menlo Park."

Menlo Park looked like a small industrial estate, with an assortment of workshops and houses. This photograph, taken in about 1880—four years after Edison moved there—shows the machine shop and laboratory, and the glassblower's house. The glassblower was a key member of the light bulb inventing team.

THE TELEPHONE MAN

Alexander Graham Bell (1847–1922) was born in Scotland and was the same age as Edison. His father taught people with hearing difficulties, and he, too, became an expert in speech and hearing. In 1870, the Bell family moved to Canada, after two sons died of tuberculosis. Aleck (as he was usually called) survived the disease, and in 1872, he moved to Boston, Massachusetts, where he taught at a school for the deaf. Bell's telephone made him famous. He later invented wax records, kept on working with the deaf, and built several flying machines, among other inventions.

The Telephone Wars

Edison drew on his **telegraph** experience to improve Bell's telephone. By the spring of 1877, he had invented a **microphone** and **transmitter,** containing tiny specks of **carbon.** The new device made the voice louder and clearer. Edison also worked out how to boost the electrical signals, increasing the range of the telephone from a few miles to hundreds of miles.

This photograph, taken in April 1878, shows Edison (seated) with Charles Batchelor and the "speaking phonograph." Within two years of Bell's first telephone, Edison and his team had built the first machine able to record and replay sound. Batchelor, a British engineer, was a key member of the group that invented the phonograph.

Western Union bought his improved telephone for $100,000, which Edison asked for in seventeen yearly installments! It was advertised as Western Union's brightest new invention, a super-telegraph for sending messages spoken by an operator. No one thought of putting phones into people's homes. Houses had no electricity.

Edison was able to prove that his "loud-speaking telephone" was better than Bell's, at a gathering of American scientists. He and Bell sat side by side while their phones were demonstrated. From Edison's, everyone heard Charles Batchelor reciting nursery rhymes and loudly singing "John Brown's Body." Bell's phone could be heard only by people sitting close by.

There were many legal battles over the telephone and its various improvements. Despite their rivalry, Edison and Bell became colleagues and friends. Each appreciated what the other had done.

Working with Edison

At Menlo Park, life revolved around the **laboratory,** with its friendly—but often frenzied—atmosphere. Edison tirelessly tried new ideas, asking his technicians to make new and odd pieces of equipment. If he got stuck on one invention, he would switch to another until the first problem solved itself. He kept a thick yellow-paged notebook in his jacket pocket, and would often stop in the middle of a conversation or a meal to scribble a note or draw a rough sketch of some new gadget. From the age of 30, he filled more than 3,000 notepads!

Edison welcomed journalists to Menlo Park. He teased them with stories about how he might one day "extract the sun's energy from cucumbers."

Edison and workers at Menlo Park were photographed in February 1880. Edison was a hard worker all his life, and he expected his employees to work hard, too. As Menlo Park grew into the world's first industrial research center, managing the tasks done by the various specialist workers became more demanding. Edison could no longer do everything himself.

FAMILY LIFE

Edison was a typical family man of his time. His home and work lives were separate. Mary Edison ran the house at Menlo Park, though the Edisons were able to afford housemaids as they grew richer. Edison worked long hours, and some nights never came home at all until daybreak. He enjoyed playing with his children, but had few hobbies. Musical concerts bored him, and trips to the city were more likely to be for business than for shopping or the theater.

In Edison's words:

"Very often I will work at a thing and get where I can't see anything more of it, and just put it aside and go at something else; and the first thing I know, the very idea I wanted will come to me. Then I drop the other and go back and work it out."

Recording Sound

Ever since the early days of photography in the 1820s, scientists had wondered if sounds could be recorded, like pictures. Sounds traveled through air as **vibrations.** These vibrations could be changed into electrical signals in the telephone. Could these same vibrations cut patterns in paper or metal? If so, they would create a recording.

Fresh from working on the telephone, Edison managed to record the clicks from a **telegraph.** He then tried speaking into a thin sheet of rubbery material, called a **diaphragm,** which vibrated as he spoke and moved a needle along a strip of paper. The needle made marks in the paper. By pulling the paper back the other way, Edison hoped to "replay" his voice.

The recording telephone

His first recording, of "Halloo!," was too fuzzy to be heard, but by midsummer 1877, he felt he was on the right track. Somehow, news leaked out. Magazines announced that Edison was about to unveil a "recording telephone." It could mean the end of books and letter-writing!

Inside Menlo Park, Edison decided to try recording onto a metal cylinder, instead of paper. John Kruesi assembled the machine, without knowing what it was for. In December, the "phonograph," or "sound-writer," was ready.

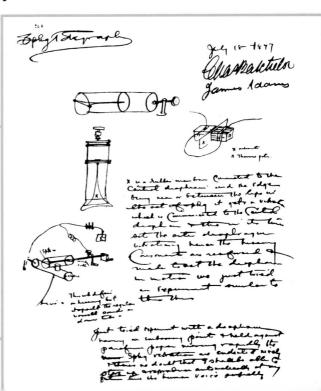

Edison made this sketch of his first phonograph in the summer of 1877. He filled notebooks with drawings, as he followed up new lines of research, spurred on by constant curiosity. Edison sold his first phonographs as public amusements. Crowds packed halls to listen to voices, music, barking dogs, steam trains—any sound that could be recorded.

In Edison's words:

"I've made a good many machines, but this is my baby, and I expect it to grow up to be a big feller and support me in my old age."

Everyone gathered around. Edison slowly recited "Mary had a little lamb," speaking into one of the phonograph's two diaphragms and slowly turning a handle, which rotated a cylinder wrapped in a sheet of tinfoil. As the cylinder turned, a needle fastened to the vibrating diaphragm tracked across the foil and cut a continuous groove.

Edison stopped speaking, moved the cylinder back to the start, and placed the second needle into the groove. He turned the handle again. There was silence, then the diaphragm began to flutter. From the machine came a faint, crackling voice: "Mary had a little lamb…."

Edison astonishes the world

"Everybody was astonished," commented Edison. Mary, Edison's wife, and other members of the team jostled to hear and try the wonderful new machine. Edison sang into it. Others recited poetry or played musical instruments.

Within the week, he was in New York City with the machine under his arm, selling it. By February 1878, he had **patented** not only the cylinder phonograph, but also ideas for recording on discs and for making copies of records.

Edison was on every newspaper's front page. He met America's top scientists, and even went to the White House to meet President Rutherford B. Hayes, who insisted his wife come from her bed after midnight to listen to the phonograph. It was almost four in the morning before Edison left.

The phonograph was the invention that Edison himself most enjoyed playing around with. He knew it was going to be a success, but imagined that it would be bought mostly by businesses as an office tool. When he first demonstrated the machine, he never dreamed that most phonograph records would be of music.

The Glowing Bulb

Edison was already thinking about another invention that would be even more revolutionary. The sun still ruled the working day; all over the world, people had to stop work at sunset. Few cities had gaslights, and most homes and streets fell dark.

Edison knew that the power of electricity could change this. There was already a form of electric light, called the **arc lamp.** It sent a brilliant spark between two pieces of **carbon.** This was fine for displays, but blinding for ordinary use. "Arc-candles" glowed, but for only two hours. Gas lamps burned for as long as gas kept hissing through the pipes.

How to make a light bulb?

Edison set out to read all he could about electric light. He talked to other scientists about the problem—there was much to learn.

Ever since the 1840s, people had tried passing electric **current** through glass bulbs, from which all the air was pumped out to leave a **vacuum** inside. As the current heated up a **filament**—a thin strip of paper or carbon inside the bulb—it got hot and gave out light. None of these electric lamps really worked. They either glimmered too faintly or burned out almost at once.

In 1878, Edison took a trip to the West to observe an eclipse of the sun. It gave him the opportunity to exchange ideas with other scientists who gathered in Wyoming with their telescopes, cameras, and other equipment. In this group photograph, taken during the trip, Edison is second from the right. The trip started him thinking about energy and light.

City streets were first lit by gas lamps in 1807, when Pall Mall in London was lit by gas. This picture of the Thames embankment in London is from the 1890s, by which time nearly every big city was gas-lit, as were many homes. Lamplighters went around at dusk to light the gas burners. Edison's electric light was about to make the hissing gas lamp a thing of the past.

Edison's bid for fame

Europe's **pioneer** of electric light was Joseph Swan of Britain. Now, Edison boldly announced that he was the leader of electric light research in the United States. Others might fail, but he would succeed!

It was a daunting task. He had to design a small but strong glass bulb that was airless inside, find a filament that would glow brightly but not burn through, and work out how to supply enough electric current to light not one bulb, but thousands!

Edison had no doubts that he would make the bulb. He was already planning to wire up houses to a central **generating** station, and was thinking up ways of charging people for the electricity they used.

The team began working furiously to make electric light. Edison even hired a "college man," mathematician Francis Upton, to help with calculations. He was determined to make history.

JOSEPH SWAN

Joseph Swan (1828–1914) was born in Sunderland, in northeast England. He worked for a photographic manufacturer and invented the bromide paper still used today to make prints of photographs. As early as 1860, he made an electric light bulb that used **battery** power, but had problems getting a proper vacuum inside the glass bulb, and air made the paper filament burn too fast. Swan went on improving his bulb into the 1880s. His idea was basically the same as Edison's, but it was Edison who took the bulb from the workbench into people's homes.

Menlo Park Lights Up

Through most of 1879, Edison and his team made and tested hundreds of glass bulbs and materials for **filaments.** They spent many hours peering at tiny glowing threads of **carbon** and metal. Even Edison complained that his eyes ached after seven hours at the workbench.

Things began to progress after Edison acquired the latest air pump, which was much better at sucking out air from inside the bulbs. Now that he could guarantee a near-perfect **vacuum,** Edison had high hopes for his latest filament—cotton sewing thread that was gently burned to coat it with carbon.

Switching on

It took two nights and a day to make the first tiny filament. Charles Batchelor carried it to the glassblower, but just as they were about to fit the thread into the bulb, it snapped! So they made another. It was fitted, air was pumped from the bulb, and the bulb was sealed. Wires were attached and Edison switched on the electric **current.** The bulb lit up.

This is a replica of Edison's first successful light bulb. The key to success was finding a filament that would glow inside the glass bulb without burning out completely. Edison and his team tried hundreds of times before they found a filament that would last many hours, making the bulb a practical source of electric light.

It was a wonderful moment. Everyone gazed in delight, and waited. On October 22, 1879, the bulb burned all day. A second bulb burned for 40 hours. Menlo Park was soon a blaze of lights, lit by bulbs of different shapes and sizes, hanging from wires strung between the trees, houses, and workshops.

The world comes to Edison

At night, the lights could be seen from miles away. People came hurrying to see Menlo Park lit up. It was a new wonder of the world.

Edison invited a *New York Herald* journalist to come and see his electric light marvel. On December 21, 1879, the story filled a whole page of the newspaper. "The Great Inventor's Triumph in Electric Illumination" electrified the nation, and news quickly spread around the world. Edison threw open his doors as special trains carried sightseers to view the lights of Menlo Park, which now boasted a restaurant lit by electric lamps. Edison declared proudly that no one would use candles from now on, except as a luxury on special occasions!

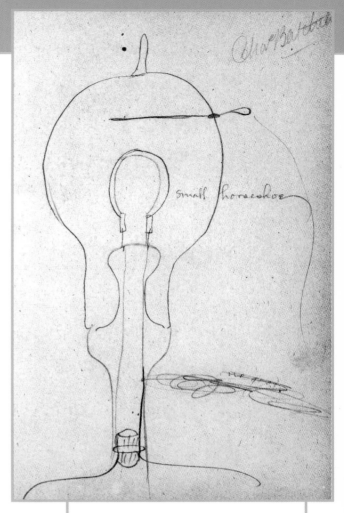

In his notebook, Edison sketched the various light bulbs made and tested at Menlo Park, noting how each filament was made and how it performed. He went on improving his bulb through the winter of 1879 and into 1880, determined to make an electric light system reliable enough to light an entire city.

In Edison's words:

Watching the second bulb burn hour after hour, Edison was jubilant. *"I think we've got it,"* he said. *"If it can burn 40 hours, I can make it last a hundred."*

Switching On

In Britain, Joseph Swan heard the news of Edison's triumph with mixed feelings. The two inventors were suspicious of one another at first, but they soon joined forces to keep their ideas from being stolen by latecomers.

Edison was already at work on development and "spin-offs," such as new bulb shapes, screw fittings, and more efficient machines to make electricity. Already, copies of his light bulb were being offered by competitors. "I always expected them," he said, "and there will be more like them."

The bulb was just the start. He had set his sights on a much bigger target: lighting the world.

Spreading the light

Edison's team went on improving the light bulb. They tested new **filaments,** and in 1880, found that bamboo burned longer than **carbon** thread. In 1881, the world's first electrically lit factory, a printing works, used Edison's bulbs. The factory had its own

steam-driven **generator.** But this was not enough for Edison. He had to think big, to make electricity at least as cheap as gas.

Into the city

In 1881, Edison moved to New York City to plan the world's first electricity power station. He planned to divide the city into sections, with each section to be linked by feeder wires to the main generator.

Edison could not just plug in to get electricity for his inventions. He had to generate his own power. This was his first generator, known as "Long-Waisted Mary Ann." A steam engine drove a pulley-belt system, which rotated a coil within the magnetic field of a large magnet. The current was then drawn off through wires attached to "brushes."

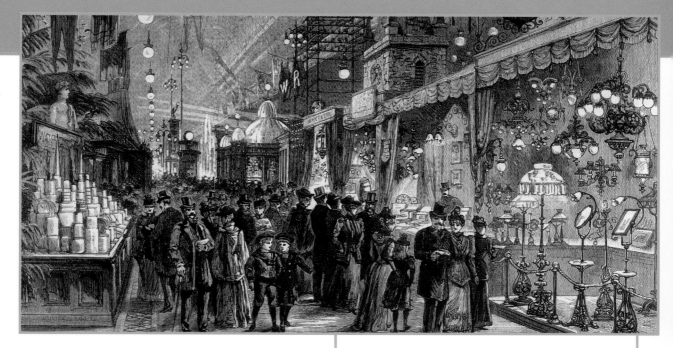

No city had ever had an electricity supply system before. Edison and his team had to make everything from scratch. They designed generators; cables to carry **current** beneath the streets; junction boxes and **fuses;** and switches and **meters** to calculate how much current each house used.

Within months, Edison had built a new **dynamo,** or generator, larger than any other and twice as efficient. He worried that current would leak from the new underground cables, so he read all he could about **insulation.** He then set to work boiling large kettles filled with various mixtures. He settled on a mixture of tar boiled in linseed oil with paraffin and beeswax. Strips of cloth soaked in this mixture were wrapped around the cables, providing a tough, waterproof insulation.

This Electrical Exhibition was held at Crystal Palace, south London, in 1882. The Edison company showed off its light bulbs and its generators designed to light city streets, factories, and homes. Crowds of sightseers and prospective customers jammed the exhibitions to gaze at the dazzling marvels of electricity.

GENERATING POWER

Generators, at first called dynamos, are machines for generating electricity. They work by using the principle of **electromagnetic induction,** discovered in 1831 by Michael Faraday. A generator changes mechanical energy into electrical energy. In its simplest form, spinning a wire loop (or many loops, called a coil) within the magnetic field of a magnet will generate an electric current around the wire. Steam engines were used to drive the first big generators in the 1880s.

Lighting the World

Electricity quickly became fashionable. The banker John Pierpont Morgan was one of the first New Yorkers to light his home. His **generator** was powered by a steam boiler in the basement. When the boiler engineer went home at 11:00 P.M., the lights in the house went out!

The Edison company was growing so fast that it needed more careful money management. For this, Edison hired a young Englishman, Samuel Insull, in 1881. Insull thought the 34-year-old Edison was very untidy, with his uncombed hair, dirty shirts, and trousers "that looked as if they had been slept in." However, they got along, and Insull, who had a sharp business brain, set to raising the money Edison needed for his ambitious schemes.

Edison opened an office in New York, to keep a close eye on his new power plant. Having a city base also made it easier for him to attend meetings with bankers and business partners. By the 1880s, money matters were taking up more of his working day, leaving him less time to tinker with inventions on the workshop bench.

In 1881, Edison showed off his super-**dynamo** at the International Electrical Exposition in Paris. The dynamo was later moved to London, where it lit 3,000 street lamps, a church, and the main post office. In 1882, the Edison company demonstrated the world's first electric sign at Crystal Palace in London. It read "EDISON."

New York switches on

Five companies were scrambling to light New York City. Edison chose a site on Pearl Street for his new power station. City politicians, given an electrically lit dinner at Menlo Park, were soon won over, and the streets were dug up for Edison's cables.

The New York power station began generating on September 4, 1882. Lights came on in offices at 3:00 P.M. When a **fuse** blew, Edison, although dressed up for the occasion, took off his coat and hat to mend it. When evening came, the lights still burned, and a *New York Times* journalist wrote the next day that "it seemed almost like writing by daylight."

There was an advertising "war" between the electricity and gas companies. Customers were enticed by electrical exhibitions and street parades of men with lights on their hats. Newspaper ads claimed that electricity was much safer than gas, which could poison you or blow you up. It was even stated that electric light could cure poor eyesight! However, the risks of electric shocks were not highlighted.

Edison soon opened a second power station, in Wisconsin. It ran on water power from the Fox River and was the world's first hydroelectric plant.

In January 1883, the Pearl Street power station was supplying 231 customers; the number doubled by August. Light bulbs lasted 400 hours, with better ones being introduced all the time. Edison could walk the streets of New York at dusk and watch his electric lights being switched on. It was a real feeling of triumph.

*Gangs of workmen dug up the streets of the city to lay the new cables for the electricity supply. The cables had to be run to every building where the owner had signed up for the new power system. Each building had to be wired, often by threading electricity wires through the old gas pipes. Light fittings, switches, fuse boxes, and **meters** all had to be installed. It was a huge job.*

Man of Many Parts

Edison was busier than ever, at times too busy to follow a promising lead. In 1883, while working on the electric light, he noticed something interesting. A **current** would flow one way, but not the other, even across a **vacuum.** The flow was being caused by **electrons** (which were then unknown), and it is now called the "Edison effect." Edison noted it but did not explore it. He had missed a vital clue to modern electronics.

Edison played around with electric trains, building one which could haul twenty people. Other people were already working on electric trains, however, and again, he lost interest.

A new family

In 1884, his wife Mary died suddenly, possibly of **typhoid fever.** Edison felt the loss deeply. They had shared the

When Mina Miller became Mrs. Edison, she tried to refine her new husband's rough-and-ready manners. She pointed out that chewing tobacco and spitting on the floor were not done in polite society.

ups and downs of building the business and raising a family. Without her, he turned to his daughter, Marion, for company. Within three years, however, he married again. Mina Miller was only twenty, about half his age, and at first, her parents did not support the match. Edison taught Mina **Morse code,** so the two could exchange secret messages.

Mary Edison had let her husband work, dress, and eat as he liked, but Mina Edison thought America's most famous inventor should appear in public more respectably. She had strong views, and was a committed Christian. Edison had never taken religion very seriously, but now home life often included discussions about the existence of God and the role of science in a changing world.

Women on the move

Although his mother had been a strong influence on his education, Edison had not taken much interest in the emerging women's movement, in which women were campaigning for the right to vote and for more independence and equality. He felt that few women wanted "to get out of the beaten path." The women he met were mostly the wives of fellow scientists and bankers, workers in factories, or servants—not **radicals** and **freethinkers.**

ONGOING IMPACT   The Edison effect

The "Edison effect" was later studied by a British scientist named John Ambrose Fleming. In 1904, he made the world's first **radio valve,** which was called the diode. In 1906, the American Lee de Forest invented the triode, a valve that could **amplify,** or strengthen, signals. The triode became a key part of radio technology, heralding the arrival of television, radar, and other wonders of the electronic age.

However, in America and Europe, more women were going through school and on to skilled jobs. Many had learned to use the typewriter, which provided new job opportunities for many independent women. The world was changing for good.

Women on the switchboard

Women were also employed in the growing telephone industry. The first switchboard was made in 1877. As the telephone network grew, many women found jobs as switchboard operators, connecting callers to the right numbers. Today, telephones connect automatically.

Women were finding new jobs in the business world. Many were hired to work as switchboard operators in new telephone exchanges, like this one. Edison's own factories also employed many women.

33

Sounds in Business

Before his marriage to Mina in 1886, Edison bought a new home in West Orange, New Jersey. Glenmont was a mansion, big enough for his three children—now ages 13, 10, and 7—and his second family. He and Mina also had a daughter and two sons.

Menlo Park was abandoned. At West Orange, Edison planned a "great industrial works," where as many as 30 or 40 new projects could go on under his watchful eye. He had less time for **laboratory** work himself, because lawsuits and business took up much of his time. He was now so famous that his views on many questions were sought by journalists. Had there been TV talk shows, he would have been a regular celebrity guest!

Rights and wrongs

His fame began to go to his head. He now saw himself as the "Great Inventor," sometimes taking credit for inventions that were not his alone, and bullying smaller firms.

Edison got most things right. One thing he got wrong was whether to use **alternating current (AC)** or direct current (DC). DC flowed one way, from **generator** to lamp and then back again. It delivered a safe low **voltage** of 250 volts, but it was too weak to be sent long distances. AC flowed in pulses— first one way, building up strength, then reversing—many times a second. AC could be sent at very high voltage across long distances. Edison mistakenly claimed that AC was unsafe, and tried to get current over 800 volts banned by law.

This is probably the most famous photograph of Edison. Taken at the West Orange laboratory, New Jersey, in June 1888, it shows him contemplating the phonograph on which he had worked nonstop for several days. His friends joked that the pose made him look like the French emperor Napoleon—a comparison Edison liked!

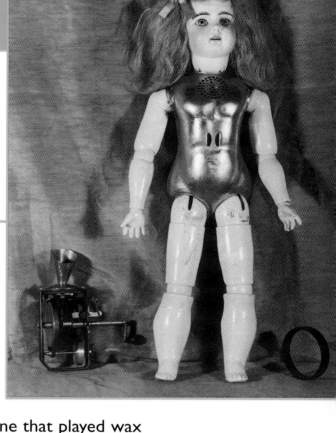

*Edison's talking doll went on sale in the 1880s. Inside the doll's body was a miniature phonographic cylinder, with a tiny trumpet **amplifier**. Turning a handle played the record, and the doll spoke.*

New sounds

Alexander Graham Bell was now working on an improved electric phonograph and suggested to Edison that they join forces. Edison said no, rudely suggesting that Bell must have stolen the idea from him.

In 1888, Edison brought out a new machine that played wax cylinders, but cylinders were on the way out. A year earlier, a German immigrant named Emile Berliner had invented a flat disc. Flat records were clearer and played for longer, but Edison went on making cylinder records into the 1920s anyway.

One gimmick using the cylinder was the Edison talking doll. It had a tiny cylinder phonograph inside it, worked by a spring motor. Girls recorded the dolls' voices by reciting nursery rhymes. However, the mechanism often worked loose during shipping.

A falling out between geniuses

Nikola Tesla (1856–1943) came to the U.S. from Croatia in 1884. He invented an improved electric motor for use with AC in 1888 and sold it to the company run by George Westinghouse. Tesla briefly worked for Edison but left, complaining that Edison had cheated him of a $50,000 bonus for improving the **dynamo.** When Tesla asked for the money, Edison said he'd been joking! In 1912, Tesla refused to share that year's **Nobel prize** for physics with Edison. Neither ever won the coveted prize.

SOUNDS FAMOUS

Famous people were invited to record their voices for posterity. It is thanks to Edison that we can listen to Queen Victoria, the poet Robert Browning, the explorer Henry Stanley, and others. Edison sent the famous Russian writer Leo Tolstoy a recording machine to help him dictate letters, but Tolstoy found it too slow and awkward.

Moving Pictures

The Edison General Electric Company was formed in 1889. Three years later, it became General Electric, which grew to be one of the giants of U.S. industry in the twentieth century. Edison was no longer "the chief," but the company gave him money for research and a new interest—moving pictures.

In 1878, a British photographer named Eadweard Muybridge took still photos of people and animals in motion, mounted them on a spinning frame, and projected the moving pictures onto a screen. Edison saw Muybridge's "zoopraxiscope" early in 1888, and decided to go one step further.

Edison worked in the laboratory whenever he could—it was where he was happiest. Every day, he went around to the different departments at West Orange, seeing how work was progressing on various projects. Pictures like this made him famous all over the world as the "Great Inventor."

Making movies

Edison picked William Dickson, a Scot, to help him make the first practical movie-film camera and **projector.** The camera was called the kinetograph. It used the new **celluloid** film strip just invented by George Eastman. Dickson's great idea was to make tiny holes along both sides of the film, so it ran smoothly over notched wheels inside the camera and projector. Modern 35 millimeter film is basically the same.

In the **laboratory** yard, the team built the world's first film studio. It was painted black inside and out and nicknamed the "Black Maria." The roof let in daylight, and the whole building could be rotated to catch the best angle of the sun to illuminate the performers as the camera filmed them.

The first projector was a **peepshow** machine, which Edison called the kinetoscope. It was unveiled in 1893, and a year later, ten "pay to peep" machines opened to the public in New York City. Crowds jammed the hall to glimpse the flickering 90-second films.

Dickson made an improved camera that shot talking pictures—the "kinetophonograph." But the sounds and pictures were not always in step, and if the actors were too far away, their voices faded into silence. Edison put his money into silent pictures, with words printed on the screen. For more than 30 years, silent movies reigned supreme.

Edison was not alone in the race to make movies. In 1890, a British inventor, William Friese-Greene, **patented** a movie camera that used the same strip film as Edison bought from Eastman. Friese-Greene wrote to Edison about his invention but received no reply. Edison met a French inventor, Étienne Marey, in Paris, and was impressed by his "photographic gun." In 1895, brothers Louis and Auguste Lumière gave their first cinema show in Paris. They showed several short films of ordinary events, such as a train arriving at a station.

The Edison kinetoscope was a peepshow machine. The customer peered in through the eyepiece on top to watch the film, which was looped over small reels. Each picture frame was about one inch (25 millimeters) wide.

In Edison's words:

Edison believed *"that a large part of education in coming generations will not be by books but by moving pictures."*

Last Years

Edison was now so rich that even though he lost a fortune in the 1890s on a mining venture, he was still a very rich man. His idea had been to use magnets to separate iron from iron **ore,** but new iron ore finds in Minnesota led to a crash in the price of iron, and the Edison iron mills shut down.

By 1900, Edison's most inventive years were behind him. However, he was still interested in new technology, such as **radio,** air travel, and cars. Henry Ford, the American car **pioneer** who produced the first factory-built family car, said he copied Edison's ideas on his new car assembly lines. Edison also designed new **batteries** for Ford cars. Close friends, Edison and Ford took summer camping trips together for many years.

In 1914, the West Orange factory burned down. Mina Edison helped her husband salvage papers from the wreckage of his office. He was back at work the next day. Film production began again within 24 hours, and the factory was rebuilt in six months.

Edison (right) and Ford, two of the most famous names in American industry, were good friends. Edison was sixteen years older than Ford, but he admired the younger man's energy and enterprise. The Ford Motor Company, founded in 1903, was the first to mass-produce cars using the assembly-line system.

Never give up

Then came World War I, from 1914 to 1918. Asked to help the U.S. Navy, Edison produced chemicals and batteries for submarines. He offered many inventions—robot exploding boats, torpedoes, periscopes, and an electrical "stun-gun"—but the Navy refused them all. The military, Edison decided, disliked interference from civilians!

Edison never retired. In his 80s, he tested thousands of plants to find a new source of rubber. He chose goldenrod, but it was never needed, because in the 1920s and 30s, synthetic (factory-made) rubber became easier to make.

Old age

Edison was so famous that all kinds of stories were told about him. Most showed his practical down-to-earth side. One night Mrs Edison came over to the **laboratory** to rescue their teenage son Charlie, who had fallen asleep on the floor. She scolded her husband for spitting on the floor; he replied that it was easier to hit than a spittoon – the dish used for the purpose in those days!

Edison was rarely ill, despite his long and erratic working hours. He never ate uncooked foods, fearing germs, and believed most people ate and slept too much. His deafness saved him, he said, from 'many interruptions and much nervous strain'.

Edison was flattered to see a model of his laboratory in Henry Ford's museum at Dearborn, Michigan. He commented wryly that the real-life laboratory floor was much dirtier! He enjoyed his fame, but hated banquets with speeches he could not hear. Although he briefly considered the notion of a 'psychic **telegraph**' to contact the spirits of the dead, he remained unconvinced by religion, despite his wife Mina's beliefs.

In August 1931 he became ill, and took to his bed. He died on 18 October aged 84. Three days later electric lights in streets and buildings across America were switched off or dimmed to mark his passing. For a moment, all was dark – as the night world had always been, until Edison switched on the light.

For his concrete house, Edison developed cement furniture. This cement cabinet, decorated in the ornate style of the time, was designed to hold a phonograph.

CONCRETE HOUSES

Edison switched his iron-mill technology to making cement. He wanted to make cheap, concrete homes for slum families. There were concrete stairs and decorations in his trial house, which took six days to dry. The idea did not catch on with the public, although factory-built concrete 'prefabs' (short for 'pre-fabricated') were widely built in Britain after World War II (1939–1945).

Edison's Legacy

During Edison's lifetime, the world changed at incredible speed. He had grown up in a world of candles, oil lamps, and horse-drawn buggies. No one had ever heard his own voice reproduced, or listened to recorded music. Edison gave the world electric lights and power at the flick of a switch. He was part of the beginning of the record and film industries. More than any other inventor, he helped to create the modern world.

His was an age in which people first drove in motor cars, listened to the **radio,** went to the movies, and flew in planes. In cities, skyscrapers towered high above streets blazing with lights and signs. The U.S. became the powerhouse of the industrial world, its assembly lines producing more in an hour than an older workshop could make in a month. Such technological advances changed the lives of millions of people. Their homes, jobs, and entertainments were very different from those of their parents.

Star scientist

Edison became a celebrity, as no scientist or engineer before had been. Self-taught, he was a perfect example for others who asked: "If he can do it, why not me?"

Edison believed in progress. He seldom asked if something could be done, only, "How?" His determination, his stream of new ideas, and his bold use of bankers' money to fund new projects, made him a model for other **pioneers.** He was no academic, shut away in a university. He was out in the real world, making things people wanted.

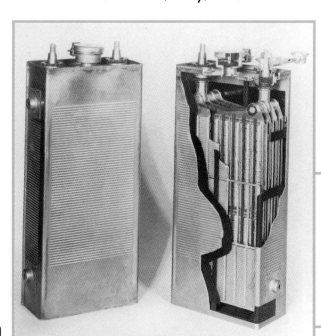

*Edison designed this storage **battery** in 1902, for use in cars. He had become interested in the car industry through his friendship with Henry Ford. He also developed batteries for submarines.*

*Even in his 80s, Edison went on working. His notebook was never far from his hand. He liked to sit in his **laboratory,** thinking and scribbling notes and sketches for new inventions.*

Team leader

Just as important was Edison's influence on business. Menlo Park was the first "research and development" organization. Today, every company relies on its team of "R and D" whiz kids to turn new ideas into new products.

Edison was also one of the first employers to hand questionnaires to job-seekers. Few questions had much to do with the work, but Edison believed they helped select the right people. Here, too, he was ahead of his time. Such aptitude tests are common in the workplace today.

His most famous remark was that "genius is one percent inspiration and **99** percent perspiration," meaning that nothing gets done without hard work. That was the way his team worked, getting the floor dirty with experiment after experiment. Edison also pointed out that of many inventions, only a very few are ever used.

Because Edison had no qualifications, some scientists snobbishly laughed at him. After all, he jumped from one project to another, instead of spending years on research. Wiser scientists, though, had only to switch on a light to be reminded of Edison's achievements.

After Edison

Journalists often asked Edison what the future would be like. With the horrors of World War I fresh in mind, he prophesied that future wars would be fought by machines. He feared the spread of terror weapons such as poison gas and flamethrowers.

In every other respect, Edison was an **optimist.** He foresaw a new world run by electricity, with labor-saving gadgets at work and in the home. Machines would do routine jobs, so people would work shorter hours and enjoy more leisure time. Electricity would free women, in particular, from the daily drudgery of washing and cleaning.

The pace of change

By the time Edison died, the modern world was taking shape. He lived just long enough to watch the first talking films. Television began in the 1930s, after his death. Radar, jet engines, and ballistic missiles were invented. Antibiotics and other revolutionary medical treatments came in the 1940s. Electronic computers appeared at the end of World War II in 1945, the war of tanks and aircraft that Edison had predicted years before.

Edison was quick to see how electric lights could be used in advertising. His electric signs were the forerunners of the dazzling neon displays in a modern city.

Today, scientists are discovering the secrets of genes, and people have been to the moon. Edison would be delighted. Our worries about global warming and the energy crisis would not scare him, for he believed people could always find solutions to problems by setting their minds to it.

A new world

The new technology, which Edison helped create, spread to every continent, producing a "global" culture.

Edison saw his business grow from a small workshop to a huge **corporation.** This pattern has been repeated many times, so that today there are multinational companies richer than many countries.

The electronics **pioneer** Robert Millikan remembered Edison asking questions about the latest scientific developments, even in his 70s. "His ears were gone, but there had been no crystallizing of the mind, such as occurs with some of us before we are born," said Millikan. In 1922, Edison wrote in his diary of atomic energy: "It may come some day. As a matter of fact, I am already experimenting…tomorrow some discovery might be made." The chemist Otto Hahn finally split the **atom** in 1938.

The world of the 21st century would probably have come about without Edison. Other people had similar ideas, and made similar breakthroughs. He was the leading light of his times, however, in more ways than one. Were the "Great Inventor" to return, he might chuckle at a modern light bulb, so little changed from his own. Show him a CD, and he would look at it, reach for his yellow notebook—and start trying to improve it.

We use Edison's inventions all the time. Imagine living without his light bulb, or working in a world where there is no power at the flick of a switch.

Timeline

1800	First **battery** invented by Alessandro Volta in Italy.
1820	Hans Christian Oersted of Denmark discovers that a wire carrying an electric current has a magnetic field surrounding it—the principle behind the electric **generator** and electric motor.
1831	Principle of **electromagnetic induction** published by Michael Faraday in Britain.
1837	Two types of electric **telegraph** are **patented** by Cooke and Wheatstone in Britain and Samuel Morse in the United States. Morse develops **Morse code** to send messages using the new technology.
1847	Thomas Alva Edison born February 11, in Milan, Ohio.
1854	The Edisons move to Port Huron, Michigan, and the next year Al goes to school.
1859	Al starts work on the train to Detroit. Charles Darwin publishes *The Origin of Species* about evolution.
1861	First telegraph link across the United States is completed. American Civil War begins.
1862	Al writes and prints his own newspaper.
1863	Edison leaves home to work as a telegrapher.
1865	President Abraham Lincoln is assassinated. American Civil War ends.
1868	Edison moves to Boston, Massachusetts; invents vote recorder.
1869	The first **railroad** across the United States is completed.
1869-70	Edison gives up telegraph work to become an inventor. Moves to New York, invents and sells stock ticker, buys workshop in Newark.
1871	Edison marries Mary Stilwell. His mother, Nancy, dies.
1874	Edison invents quadruplex telegraph, capable of sending four messages at once.
1876	Alexander Graham Bell invents the telephone. Edison moves to Menlo Park, which he makes into the world's first industrial research center.
1877	Edison invents the phonograph.
1879	Edison develops a generator/electric motor; invents electric light.
1882	Edison opens New York City power station.
1884	Edison's first wife, Mary, dies.
1886	Edison marries Mina Miller on February 24. Moves to West Orange, New Jersey.

1888	George Eastman develops rolled strips of film for cameras. Edison's team invents the kinetograph (camera) and kinetoscope (viewer).
1895	Auguste and Louis Lumière present the first public movies in Paris, France.
1901	Guglielmo Marconi sends first **radio** signals across the Atlantic using wireless telegraphy.
1908	Henry Ford begins selling his cheap Model T family car.
1912	Edison designs battery for starter on Ford cars.
1914	West Orange factory burns down and is rebuilt six months later.
1915	Edison is appointed president of the U.S. Naval Consulting Board.
1917	The United States enters World War I.
1920s	Edison still working, though now "retired." Radio broadcasts of news and entertainment programs begin. First talking pictures at the movies.
1927	Charles Lindbergh makes first solo flight across the Atlantic. First transatlantic telephone call.
1931	Edison dies at his home in West Orange on October 18.

More Books to Read

Adair, Gene. *Thomas Edison: Inventor.* Berkeley Heights, N.J.: Enslow Publishers, Inc., 1996.

Linder, Greg. *Thomas Edison.* Mankato, Minn.: Capstone Press, 1999.

Sabin, Louis. *Thomas Alva Edison: Young Inventor.* Mahwah, N.J.: Troll Communications, L.L.C., 1997.

Glossary

alternating current (AC) electric current that rapidly changes direction

amplify to make stronger

arc lamp electric light that gives a very bright light; invented in 1812 by Humphry Davy

atom smallest part of an element that has all its properties

battery device for storing electricity; it works when metals react with liquids to produce a current between metal plates called electrodes

carbon natural substance that takes many forms, including diamonds, coal, and soot

celluloid first artificial plastic, invented in 1869; used to make photographic film

commerce business; making and selling goods or services

Congress lawmaking body of the United States government

corporation large business organization

current flow of electricity; electrons move along a suitable conductor, such as a metal wire

diaphragm thin, bendy sheet or plate that vibrates

dynamo old name for a generator for making electricity, usually DC (direct current)

electromagnetic induction principle by which an electric current can be produced by spinning a wire coil in the magnetic field of a magnet; discovered by Michael Faraday in 1831

electromagnetism force produced when an electric current flows through a coil of wire

electron part of an atom that orbits the nucleus and carries an electrical charge

filament thin thread, such as a piece of cotton or thin wire, used in electric light bulbs

freethinker person who rejects authority and tradition, especially in religious matters

fuse safety device that burns through if an electric current is too high, breaking the circuit

generator machine for making electrical energy from mechanical energy. It can burn fuel such as coal or oil, or use the power of water, nuclear, wind, or solar energy.

insulator substance that does not allow electricity to pass through it

laboratory place where experiments are carried out

magnetism natural force that electric currents give out. Iron and other metals can also act as magnets, sticking to other metals.

meter measuring instrument, for example the type that can record flow of electricity into a house

microphone device that can "pick up" sounds (a voice, for example) and change the sound signals into electrical signals

Morse code code invented by Samuel Morse in which groups of short electrical signals (dots) and longer ones (dashes) stand for letters of the alphabet

Nobel prize annual prize for physics, chemistry, medicine, literature, economics, and work for peace

optimist someone who looks on the bright side, expecting things to get better

ore rock containing a metal

patent government grant to an inventor, giving him or her the sole right to make, use, and sell their invention for a set period of time

peepshow machine which people paid to look into and watch a short film

philosopher person who seeks wisdom and knowledge

pioneer person who is first to do something; either to settle in a new land or work in a new field of knowledge

projector machine for showing films or photographs in enlarged form on a screen, using lenses and strong lights

radical person who is in favor of far-reaching political and social change

radio sending sounds through the air electronically, without wires

telegraph communications system that works by sending electrical signals in code through wires

transmitter device for sending signals or messages

typhoid fever severe infectious fever

vacuum absence of matter; empty, airless space

valve in electronics, a device for controlling a current, letting it flow one way but not the other

vibration movement back and forth, like the fluttering of a fan

voltage push that makes an electric current flow around a circuit; measured in volts

Index